W9-BJN-520

DATE DUE

NOV 6			

Demco, Inc. 38-293

THE
NEWFOUNDLAND

by Charlotte Wilcox

Consultant:
Judi Adler
Sweetbay Newfoundlands

C A P S T O N E
H I G H / L O W   B O O K S
an imprint of Capstone Press
Mankato, Minnesota

Capstone High/Low Books are published by Capstone Press
818 North Willow Street, Mankato, Minnesota 56001
http://www.capstone-press.com

Library of Congress Cataloging-in-Publication Data
Wilcox, Charlotte.
    The Newfoundland/by Charlotte Wilcox.
    p. cm.—(Learning about dogs)
    Includes bibliographical references (p. 45) and index.
    Summary: Introduces the history, development, uses, and care of this
dog breed, known for lifesaving and search-and-rescue work.
    ISBN 0-7368-0160-X
    1. Newfoundland dog—Juvenile literature. [1. Newfoundland dog.
2. Dogs.] I. Title. II. Series: Wilcox, Charlotte. Learning about dogs.
SF429.N4W55   1999
636.73—dc21
                                                            98-37632
                                                               CIP
                                                                AC

Editorial Credits
Timothy Halldin, cover designer; Sheri Gosewisch and Kimberly Danger, photo
researchers

Photo Credits
Archive Photos, 15
Cheryl A. Ertelt, 23, 28, 32, 40
John Elk III, 27
Kent and Donna Dannen, cover, 4, 6, 9, 10, 12, 19, 24, 30
Mark Raycroft, 16, 20, 39
Unicorn Stock Photos/Dick Young, 35; Ronald E. Partis, 36

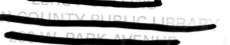

Table of Contents

Quick Facts about the Newfoundland

Description

Height: Male Newfoundlands (NOO-fuhn-luhndz)
stand about 28 inches (71 centimeters) tall.
Females stand about 26 inches
(66 centimeters) tall. Height is measured
from the ground to the withers. The
withers are the tops of the shoulders.

Weight: Male Newfoundlands weigh 130 to
150 pounds (59 to 68 kilograms).
Females weigh 100 to 120 pounds
(45 to 54 kilograms).

Physical features:	Newfoundlands are among the largest dog breeds. They have large heads with small ears. Their hair is long and can be wavy or smooth.
Colors:	Newfoundlands most commonly are black, brown, or gray. Some have white areas on their chins, chests, toes, or the tips of their tails. Newfoundlands also can be white with black markings.

Development

Place of origin:	Newfoundlands came from the island of Newfoundland in eastern Canada.
History of breed:	Newfoundlands developed from dogs from Europe. European fishermen brought these dogs to Canada. These dogs from Europe bred with native North American dogs.
Numbers:	The American Kennel Club registers about 2,800 Newfoundlands each year. To register means to record a dog's breeding record with an official club. The Canadian Kennel Club registers about 700 Newfoundlands each year.

Uses

Newfoundlands do lifesaving in water. They also do land search-and-rescue work. They also can pull carts and sleds. Newfoundlands make good family pets.

Chapter 1
Built for Hard Work

Newfoundland dogs can save people's
lives. They have a lifesaving instinct. An
instinct is a behavior that animals do naturally.
An instinct is not learned. Hunting dogs chase
birds by instinct. Herding dogs round up
livestock by instinct.

Instinct directs Newfoundlands what to do
in dangerous situations. They are the only
breed that has natural lifesaving ability listed
in its standard. Standards are descriptions
written by breed clubs. Standards list the ideal
qualities of an official dog breed.

Newfoundlands' body features help them
save lives. Newfoundlands are one of the

**Newfoundlands are one of the largest, strongest
dog breeds.**

largest and strongest dog breeds. They have good eyesight and excellent hearing. Many Newfoundlands are excellent swimmers. They have two layers of hair. The inner layer is soft and fuzzy. The outer layer is long and sleek. Water does not go through the outer layer. This layer keeps Newfoundlands' skin dry when they swim. Newfoundlands also have webbed feet. The extra skin connecting their toes helps make them good swimmers.

Hauling and Carrying

Newfoundlands can do many jobs. They can pull sleds during winter. They can carry packs on their backs. People once trained Newfoundlands to walk on treadmill belts to power machinery. Teams of Newfoundlands once hauled wood out of forests. These strong dogs even pulled carts from town to town without a human driver.

Island of Newfoundland

Newfoundland dogs are named after an island. The island of Newfoundland is located off the

Newfoundlands can pull carts without a human driver.

southeast coast of the Canadian province of Newfoundland. Canada is divided into provinces just as the United States is divided into states.

The island of Newfoundland has 8,500 miles (13,679 kilometers) of ocean shoreline. This island is surrounded by the Atlantic Ocean. Until the 1900s, most people who worked and lived on the island of Newfoundland were fishermen. There are many lakes and ponds on the island. Thousands of miles of rivers and streams cross the island. Newfoundland dogs came from this island.

Newfoundlands came from the island of Newfoundland in eastern Canada. They are excellent swimmers.

Chapter 2
The Beginnings of the Breed

The early history of Newfoundland and its dogs is not clear. The first people to live on what is now the island of Newfoundland were native North Americans. Historians think these native peoples first lived on the island thousands of years ago. They were related to today's Inuit (IN-oo-it) people. Inuit people now live in Alaska, Canada, Greenland, and Siberia.

The Great Pyrenees and Newfoundland dog breeds look alike. But these two breeds are probably not related.

Inuit people have raised dogs for thousands of years. They use Siberian Husky dogs to hunt, pull, and carry things. Some people think the Siberian Husky is one ancestor of the Newfoundland. An ancestor is a family member from long ago.

Norse People

Historians also think that Norse (NORSS) dogs and Mastiffs are Newfoundland ancestors. The Norse people arrived at what is now the island of Newfoundland about 1,000 years ago. The Norse people came from the area that is now Scandinavia. This area includes Norway, Sweden, Denmark, Iceland, and Greenland.

Some Norse sailors had tried to sail from Iceland to Greenland in the year A.D. 986. A storm began during the trip. The storm blew their ship off course. These sailors landed on what is now the island of Newfoundland.

These Norse sailors returned to Iceland after the storm. They told other people about

Inuit people use Siberian Huskies to pull sleds. Siberian Huskies may be related to Newfoundlands.

the island. The explorer Leif Eriksson heard these stories. He wanted to visit this island.

Eriksson and his men landed on what is now the island of Newfoundland about the year 1000. They were the first Europeans to explore the island.

Some Norse people decided to move to the island. They brought their families, livestock, and dogs with them. The Norse dogs had thick

Newfoundlands' thick hair helps to protect them from cold temperatures.

hair to protect them from cold weather. Their hair came in many color combinations. Many of them had white markings. Others were all black. The Norse dogs bred with the dogs that belonged to the native people of the island.

The Norse people stayed on the island for only a few years. They wrote about the native people and their dogs. They wrote that the native dogs were good swimmers. Nobody is sure why the Norse people left the island. No other Europeans lived there for centuries afterward.

More European Visitors

Fishermen from Spain also traveled to Newfoundland nearly 1,000 years ago. They visited the island after the Norse people lived there. The Spanish fishermen did not stay on the island. They caught fish and took them back to Spain to sell. These fishermen noticed the native dogs. They also brought their own dogs to Newfoundland.

The dogs from Spain were called Mastiffs. These are large, heavy dogs. Mastiffs are native to Europe and Asia. They are ancestors of many large breeds. Mastiffs bred with native and Norse dogs on Newfoundland.

Explorers from England first came to Newfoundland in 1497. Captain John Cabot claimed the island as territory for England. He named the area Newfoundland from his description of the territory as "new founde lande."

People from Portugal sailed to the island of Newfoundland in 1500. Soon people from many European countries visited the island. They found plenty of fish in Newfoundland's waters.

English people moved to the island of Newfoundland in the late 1500s. They built homes and towns. They built factories to prepare fish for sale. Newfoundland became an important world fishing center.

Fishermen's Dogs

Dogs were important on fishing boats. They helped fishermen with the nets used to catch fish. The nets hung from ropes into the water. Fish swam into the nets. The fishermen pulled the ropes to move the nets onto the boats. Dogs pulled ropes and nets with their mouths.

Dogs helped fishermen in other ways. Dogs could swim faster than people. They could see underwater better than people could. They also could catch escaping fish in their mouths in shallow water.

Newfoundlands have webbed feet. This feature helps make many Newfoundlands excellent swimmers.

Ships from many countries sailed to the island of Newfoundland. Sailors and passengers saw the helpful dogs of Newfoundland. Soon, ships from many different countries had a Newfoundland dog on board. These big dogs went to live in countries all over the world.

Chapter 3
Heroes and Friends

Newfoundlands worked on ships during the sailing age. This period lasted from about 1600 to 1900. Newfoundlands were good dogs to have aboard ships because they could swim well.

Newfoundlands had other qualities that suited them for life aboard ships. Newfoundlands were intelligent. They could understand what their owners expected of them. They were strong. They could carry heavy ropes and pull nets. They could even break through ice in winter. Newfoundlands were brave. Their instinct was to save lives.

People sometimes use Newfoundlands to carry packs.

Running the Lifeline

Newfoundlands had one especially important job. They carried a lifeline when a ship was in danger of sinking near shore. A lifeline was a rope sailors used during storms to connect the ship to shore. Newfoundlands carried the lifeline to the ship or the shore. The water was too cold and rough for a person to swim to shore during a storm. People on the ship used the lifeline to reach land.

People used the lifeline in two ways. Sometimes people on the ship sent the lifeline. Then the Newfoundland brought the rope to people on shore. But sometimes there was not a dog on the ship. Then people on shore sent out the lifeline. The dog carried the lifeline out to the ship.

The people on board the ship tied the lifeline to something sturdy. The people on shore tied the lifeline to a dock or rock. The people on the ship then held on to the rope and tried to pull themselves to shore. They could make it safely to shore holding the line.

Newfoundlands have saved many people from drowning.

Newfoundlands are strong and can pull heavy weights.

Newfoundlands were suited to running the lifeline. Newfoundlands had great strength and daring. The waves were rough and dangerous. Newfoundlands could see underwater. They could swim through giant waves. They even could find the ship or shore in the dark.

Newfoundland dogs rescued hundreds of people by carrying lifelines. They also rescued people on ships in other ways. They sometimes carried people to shore one at a time. People would grip the Newfoundlands' long hair. Newfoundlands even pulled small boats to shore.

Boatswain

A Newfoundland dog named Boatswain (BOHZ-uhn) accidentally changed European history. Boatswain was born on the island of Newfoundland about 1800. When Boatswain was 2 years old, someone gave him to Prince George IV of England.

One night in 1804, the prince gave a party. A man from France and a man from Prussia (PRUHSH-uh) were there. Prussia was then a powerful military state of Germany. The Frenchman had a letter in his pocket. The letter made fun of the Prussian man.

The letter fell out of the Frenchman's pocket. Boatswain noticed the letter on the floor. He picked it up and brought it to the prince. The prince read it and handed it to the Prussian. The Prussian became very angry. He went back to Prussia and told others what had happened. Prussia then decided to join England in the Napoleonic Wars (1799–1815) against France. France later lost the war at the Battle of Waterloo in 1815.

Seaman

A Newfoundland named Seaman appears in American history. Seaman was a 150-pound (68-kilogram), black Newfoundland. His owner was an army captain named Meriwether Lewis. Lewis bought Seaman in Pittsburgh, Pennsylvania, for $20.

Lewis was a leader of the famous Lewis and Clark exploration team. His partner was William Clark. Lewis and Clark's team explored parts of the Louisiana Purchase territory. The area they explored is in what are now the states of Missouri, Iowa, Nebraska, South Dakota, North Dakota, Montana, Idaho, and Oregon.

Lewis and Clark left what is now St. Louis, Missouri, in 1804. They traveled along rivers to the Pacific Ocean. The trip took more than

A statue in Oregon shows the Newfoundland that helped the Lewis and Clark exploration team.

two years. Seaman helped the team hunt for food. He also guarded their camp at night. He barked if wild animals came near.

Today, a statue stands where Lewis and Clark's group reached the Pacific Ocean. It is at Fort Clatsop near Astoria, Oregon. The statue is of Seaman, Lewis, his partner Clark, and an American Indian from the Clatsop Indian people. The Clatsop people helped the explorers at their winter camp in 1805–1806.

Chapter 4

The Newfoundland Today

Many Newfoundland dogs are family pets. Some watch over children. Some act as lifeguards. Newfoundland dogs are sometimes called Newfs or Newfies. They are very calm and friendly dogs.

Appearance

Male Newfoundlands stand about 28 inches (71 centimeters) tall. Females stand about 26 inches (66 centimeters) tall. Height is measured from the ground to the withers. The withers are the tops of the shoulders.

Black and Landseer are two Newfoundland colors. Landseer dogs are white with black markings.

Newfoundland dogs make good pets.

Males generally weigh between 130 and 150 pounds (59 to 68 kilograms). Females generally weigh between 100 and 120 pounds (45 to 54 kilograms).

Newfoundland Colors

Newfoundlands most commonly are black, brown, or gray. Some have white areas on their chins, chests, toes, or the tips of their tails.

Newfoundlands also can be white, with black markings. This color is called Landseer. It is named for Sir Edwin Henry Landseer. He was a famous London artist who painted pictures of Newfoundlands in the 1800s. Landseer Newfoundlands have a large black patch over their backs. Another black patch covers their rears and part of their tails. Their heads are either all black or black and white.

Black Paws

People train Newfoundlands to save lives. These dogs can search for lost people. They can rescue people from drowning.

One national search-and-rescue group uses only Newfoundlands. Susie Foley began the Black Paws Search, Rescue, and Avalanche Academy in 1985 in Big Fork, Montana. She named the group Black Paws in honor of the Newfoundland dogs. Newfoundlands are excellent rescue dogs because they are strong, gentle, and intelligent.

People who own Newfoundlands and want to learn about rescue work can attend Black Paws

Black Paws training teaches Newfoundlands and their owners life-saving skills.

training. Black Paws is now located in West Glacier, Montana. Black Paws has groups across the United States. There also is a Black Paws group in New Zealand.

Black Paws training teaches Newfoundlands and their owners search-and-rescue skills. They find people lost in forests, parks, or fields.

Newfoundlands learn to find the scent of people who are hurt or afraid. They learn to find people who are underwater or buried under snow.

Newfoundlands trained by Black Paws have rescued many people. Police or the FBI can request Black Paws dogs and their owners to help rescue lost or injured people. Rescue trainers teach people and their Newfoundlands about lifesaving. But many untrained Newfoundlands have rescued people because of the dogs' instincts.

Villa

Villa was a 1-year-old Newfoundland dog. Her owners named her for Villas, New Jersey, where they lived. Three little girls lived next to Villa. On February 11, 1983, the girls were playing outdoors. A terrible snowstorm began. Two girls went inside. But one girl named Andrea stayed behind. The strong wind blew her down a hill.

Andrea was buried in snow. She called out for help. Nobody could hear her except Villa.

The dog heard Andrea's voice above the wind. Villa jumped her 5-foot fence. Villa found the girl in the snow. Andrea was trapped and could not move.

Villa knew what to do. She stamped in a circle and packed down the snow. Andrea put her arms around Villa's neck. Villa then pulled Andrea free. The two struggled up the hill. They fell down many times. Each time, Villa waited for Andrea to grab on to her again. Together they finally made it home.

Newfoundlands and Sports

Newfoundlands are good swimmers. Clubs have tests where dogs swim and dive. Dogs win prizes when they swim and dive well. The dogs receive a title of honor that is added to their names. They also receive a national certificate for passing water tests.

Newfoundlands can pull people or objects in sleds or carts. People place the dogs in harnesses. Straps called traces connect the harnesses to the sleds or carts.

Newfoundlands sometimes pull people or objects in sleds or carts.

Newfoundlands also can pull people on skis. This is called skijoring.

    Many Newfoundland owners hike with their dogs. The dogs' large webbed feet make them good hikers. Newfoundlands are strong enough to carry a pack on their backs. They can hike for many hours.

Chapter 5

Owning a Newfoundland

Newfoundland puppies are small and furry. But most Newfoundlands are fully grown within a year. This large dog will shed hair and drool. Many will not stay out of the water. But many people enjoy these large, gentle dogs.

Feeding a Newfoundland

The best type of food for Newfoundlands is good-quality, ready-prepared dog food. Dog food comes in dry, semimoist, and canned forms. Semimoist means some water has been

Newfoundland puppies are small and furry.

taken out. The amount of food dogs need depends on their age and activity level. It is important to feed dogs only the food they need. Fat dogs are not healthy.

Grown Newfoundlands may eat 1 1/2 to 2 pounds (680 to 907 grams) of dry or semimoist food each day. Or, they may eat five or six cans of canned food. It is best to divide the food into two meals.

Dogs also need plenty of fresh water each day. They should drink as often as they want. This should be at least three times a day.

Grooming and Health Care

Owners should brush their Newfoundlands every day. This keeps their long hair from getting tangled. Newfoundlands shed a little hair every day. They shed large amounts once or twice a year. They need extra brushing during those times.

Newfoundlands' toenails should be kept short. Long toenails can cause foot problems in large breeds. Newfoundlands need shots every

Newfoundlands shed a little of their hair every day.

year to guard them from illnesses. They also need a checkup for worms every year.

Newfoundlands live an average of six years. But many healthy Newfoundlands can live as long as 10 to 12 years.

It is best to buy puppies from breeders. Good breeders try to raise healthy dogs. Pet stores sometimes sell dogs with health problems. Local Newfoundland clubs help people find strong, healthy dogs.

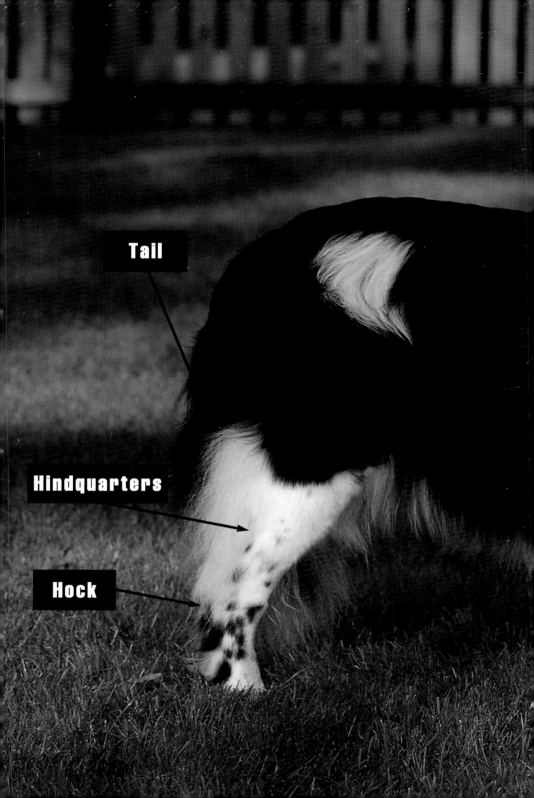

Tail

Hindquarters

Hock

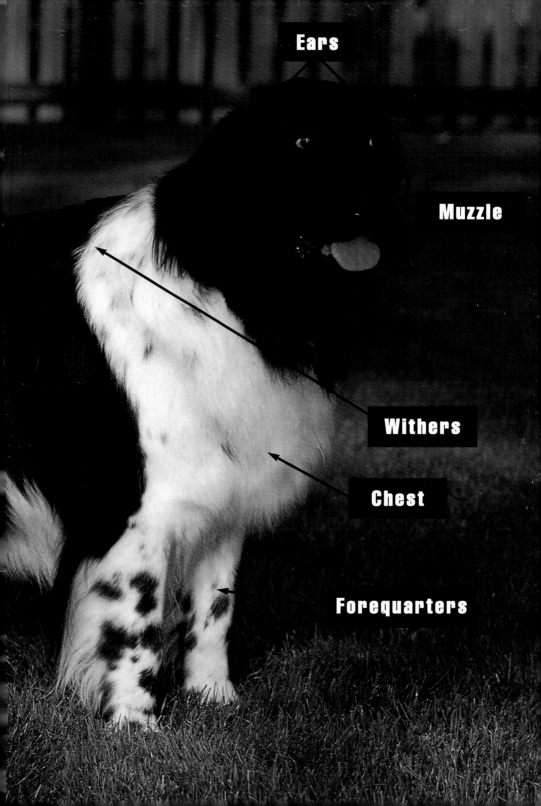

Ears

Muzzle

Withers

Chest

Forequarters

Quick Facts about Dogs

Dog Terms

A male dog is called a dog. A female dog is called a bitch. A young dog is called a puppy until it is 1 year old. A newborn puppy is called a whelp until it no longer needs its mother's milk. A family of puppies born at one time is called a litter.

Life History

Origin:	All dogs, wolves, coyotes, and dingoes descended from a single, wolf-like species. Humans trained dogs throughout history.
Types:	There are about 350 official dog breeds in the world. Dogs come in different sizes and colors. Adult dogs weigh from 2 pounds (1 kilogram) to more than 200 pounds (91 kilograms). They range from 6 inches (15 centimeters) to 36 inches (91 centimeters) tall.
Reproductive life:	Dogs mature at 6 to 18 months. Puppies are born two months after breeding. A female can have two litters per year. An average litter has three to six puppies. Litters of 15 or more puppies are possible.
Development:	Newborn puppies cannot see or hear. Their ears and eyes open one to two weeks after birth. Puppies try to walk when they are 2 weeks old. Their teeth begin to come in when they are about 3 weeks old.
Life span:	Dogs are fully grown at 2 years. They can live 15 years or longer with good care.

The Dog's Super Senses

Smell:
Dogs have a strong sense of smell. It is many times stronger than a human's. Dogs use their noses more than their eyes and ears. They recognize people, animals, and objects just by smelling them. They may recognize smells from long distances. They also may remember smells for long periods of time.

Hearing:
Dogs hear better than people do. Dogs can hear noises from long distances. They also can hear high-pitched sounds that people cannot hear.

Sight:
Dogs' eyes are farther to the sides of their heads than people's are. They can see twice as wide around their heads as people can.

Touch:
Dogs enjoy being petted more than almost any other animal. They also can feel vibrations from approaching trains or the beginning of earthquakes or storms.

Taste:
Dogs do not have a strong sense of taste. This is partly because their sense of smell overpowers their sense of taste. It also is partly because they swallow food too quickly to taste it well.

Navigation:
Dogs often can find their way home through crowded streets or across miles of wilderness without guidance. This is a special ability that scientists do not fully understand.

Words to Know

ancestor (AN-sess-tur)—a member of a person's or animal's family that lived a long time ago

Landseer (LAND-sihr)—a Newfoundland dog that is white with black markings in a special pattern

litter (LIT-ur)—a group of animals born at the same time to one mother

Mastiff (MASS-tif)—a breed of dog that is large and powerful; Mastiffs often are used for hunting, herding, or fighting.

register (REJ-uh-stur)—to record a dog's breeding record with an official club

search and rescue (SURCH and RESS-kyoo)—using dogs to find and rescue people who are lost or hurt

Siberian Husky (sye-BEER-ee-an HUHSS-kee)—a breed of dog with a thick coat; huskies were bred to pull sleds in the far North.

skijoring (SKEE-jor-ing)—a winter sport in which a person wearing skis is pulled over ice or snow by a dog

To Learn More

American Kennel Club. *The Complete Dog Book for Kids.* New York: Howell Book House, 1996.

Richards, Hedd and Del Richards. *Newfoundlands Today.* New York: Howell Book House, 1997.

Taylor, David. *Dogs.* Pockets. New York: Dorling-Kindersley, 1997.

Tucker, Michael. *Dog Training for Children and Parents.* New York: Howell Book House, 1998.

You can read articles about Newfoundlands in magazines such as *AKC Gazette*, *Dog Fancy*, *Dogs in Canada*, *Dog World*, and *Newfoundland.*

Useful Addresses

American Kennel Club
5580 Centerview Drive
Raleigh, NC 27606

Canadian Kennel Club
89 Skyway Avenue, Suite 100
Etobicoke, ON M9W 6R4
Canada

Newfoundland Club of America
Corresponding Secretary
P.O. Box 370
Green Valley, IL 61543

Newfoundland Dog Club of Canada
P.O. Box 346
New Dundee, ON N0B 2E0
Canada

Internet Sites

American Kennel Club
http://www.akc.org

Canadian Kennel Club
http://www.canadiankennelclub.com

Dogs in Canada
http://www.dogs-in-canada.com

Newfoundland Club of America
http://www.geocities.com/~newfdogclub

Newfoundland Dog Club of Canada
http://www.golden.net/~blacknita

Newfoundland Rescue Club of Canada
http://web.idirect.com/~loydex/rescue.html

Index